LIGHTNING BOLT BOOKS

Cool Sports Cars

Jon M. Fishman

Lerner Publications ◆ Minneapolis

Lerner Publications Company
A division of Lerner Publishing Group, Inc.
241 First Avenue North
Minneapolis, MN 55401 USA

For reading levels and more information, look up this title at www.lernerbooks.com.

Library of Congress Cataloging-in-Publication Data

Names: Fishman, Jon M., author.
Title: Cool sports cars / Jon M. Fishman.
Description: Minneapolis : Lerner Publications, [2019] | Series: Lightning bolt books. Awesome rides | Includes bibliographical references and index. | Audience: Ages 6–9. | Audience: Grades K to grade 3.
Identifiers: LCCN 2017044068 (print) | LCCN 2017047375 (ebook) | ISBN 9781541525108 (eb pdf) | ISBN 9781541519985 (library bound : alk. paper) | ISBN 9781541527584 (paperback : alk. paper)
Subjects: LCSH: Sports cars—Juvenile literature.
Classification: LCC TL236 (ebook) | LCC TL236 .F5725 2019 (print) | DDC 629.222—dc23

LC record available at https://lccn.loc.gov/2017044068

Manufactured in the United States of America
1-44334-34580-11/15/2017

Table of Contents

It's a Sports Car!

A sports car zooms around a bend in the road. The car is small and close to the ground. Tiny rocks fly from its spinning tires.

Sports cars can reach 60 miles (97 km) per hour in just four seconds.

Sports cars are fun to drive. Carmakers build sports cars to be fast and easy to steer. They speed up quickly and turn smoothly.

Sports cars are usually small. They don't have much room for passengers or cargo.

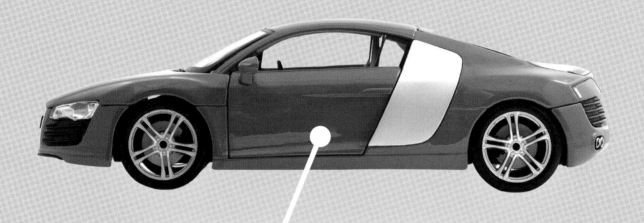

Many sports cars do not have large trunks or big back seats. Some don't have back seats at all!

Some people drive
sports cars in races.
People also drive them
to work or to school.

The Sports Car Story

Carmakers in the early twentieth century built fast cars. Fast cars could win races. Winning races was a good way for carmakers to spread the word about their cars.

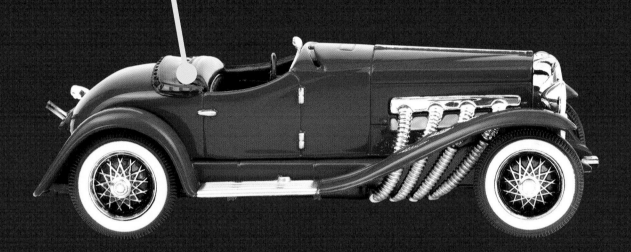

The driver sits close to the back of a sports car.

Sports cars in the 1920s had big engines. The cars had long hoods and two seats for passengers.

Sports cars became more popular after World War II (1939–1945). People loved driving the small cars and watching races.

Sports cars were popular in other countries before they became popular in the United States.

These days, sports cars come in many shapes and sizes. But some things haven't changed from the early years. Sports cars are still fast and fun to drive!

Sports Car Parts

Whoosh! A sports car rushes down a street. The car's smooth body cuts cleanly through the air. Its shape helps the car go fast.

A sports car usually has
two doors and two seats.
It has a small trunk in
the back.

Most early sports cars had soft tops.

Some sports cars are soft-tops. Lower the top, and let the wind blow through your hair!

A sports car's engine is usually in the front. It is big and powerful compared to the size of the car. That's partly why sports cars can go so fast!

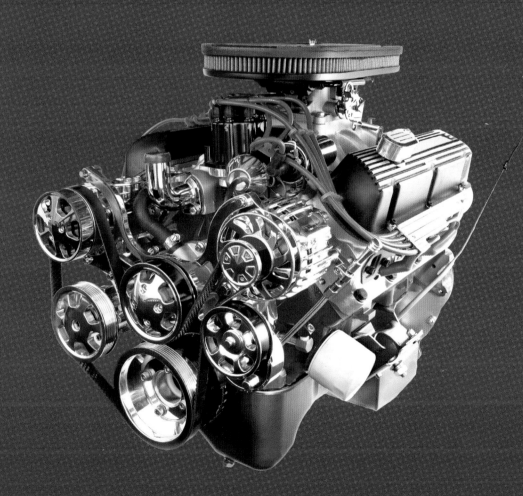

Sports Cars in Action

Sports cars rocket down a racetrack. They whiz by a crowd of people. The fans cheer and take photos.

One popular race takes twenty-four hours to complete.

Sports car races take place around the world. There are races for many types of sports cars. The races are on tracks, country roads, and even closed city streets.

People in the United States buy thousands of sports cars every year. They love driving cars built for racing. Sports cars can make any trip fun!

Sports car engines are more powerful than ever. They are also getting better at using less fuel. Sports cars will always be a thrill to drive!

Sports Car Diagram

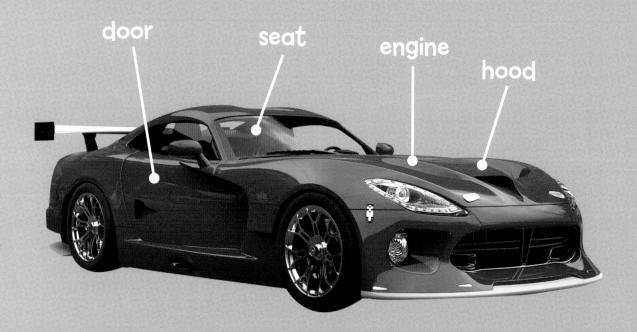

door

seat

engine

hood

Sports Car Facts

- The Rinspeed sQuba can drive on land and float on water. This sports car can also dive 33 feet (10 m) below the water's surface.

- The Mazda MX-5 Miata is the best-selling two-seat sports car in the world. Mazda had made one million Miatas by 2016.

- The Bugatti Veyron Super Sport is considered the world's fastest sports car. It has been clocked at more than 267 miles (430 km) per hour.

Glossary

body: the main outside part of a car

cargo: things carried in a vehicle

fuel: something such as oil or gas that is burned to make power

hood: the cover of a car's engine

passenger: a traveler in a vehicle

soft-top: a car with a roof made of fabric that can be lowered

trunk: the space at the rear of a car used to carry cargo

Further Reading

Boothroyd, Jennifer. *From the Model T to Hybrid Cars: How Transportation Has Changed.* Minneapolis: Lerner Publications, 2012.

Crane, Cody. *Race Cars*. New York: Children's Press, 2018.

Facts about Cars
http://www.scienceforkidsclub.com/cars.html

Parrish, Margaret, ed. *Fast Cars*. Mankato, MN: New Forest, 2012.

Rubber Band Car
http://pbskids.org/designsquad/build/rubber -band-car

Index

Photo Acknowledgments

The images in this book are used with the permission of: Vladimiroquai/Shutterstock.com, p. 2; Ermess/Shutterstock.com, p. 4; yousang/Shutterstock.com, p. 5; Andrey Lobachev/Shutterstock.com, p. 6; ermess/Shutterstock.com, p. 7; National Motor Museum/Heritage Images/Getty Images, p. 8; miroslavmisiura/Shutterstock.com, p. 9; BIPS/Getty Images, p. 10; erkanatbas/Shutterstock.com, p. 11; Hetman Bohdan/Shutterstock.com, p. 12; JULIE LUCHT/Shutterstock.com, p. 13; Sergey Kohl/Shutterstock.com, p. 14; Steve Bower/Shutterstock.com, p. 15; bonzodog/Shutterstock.com, p. 16; Stanislaw Tokarski/Shutterstock.com, p. 17; Philip Pilosian/Shutterstock.com, p. 18; Pavlo Baliukh/Shutterstock.com, p. 19; Trimitrius/Shutterstock.com, p. 20.

Front cover: ermess/Shutterstock.com.

Main body text set in Billy Infant regular 28/36. Typeface provided by SparkType.

Leading-edge
psychological tests and
c2007.

0 1341 1125235 6